THOMAS CRANE PUBLIC LIBRARY
QUINCY MA

CITY APPROPRIATION

Wisconsin

Jim Ollhoff

Visit us at
www.abdopublishing.com

Published by ABDO Publishing Company, 8000 West 78th Street, Suite 310, Edina, Minnesota 55439 USA. Copyright ©2010 by Abdo Consulting Group, Inc. International copyrights reserved in all countries. No part of this book may be reproduced in any form without written permission from the publisher. The Checkerboard Library™ is a trademark and logo of ABDO Publishing Company.

Printed in the United States.

Editor: John Hamilton
Graphic Design: Sue Hamilton
Cover Illustration: Neil Klinepier
Cover Photo: iStock Photo
Interior Photo Credits: Alamy, AP Images, Corbis, David Olson, Edward Marek, Fort Crawford Museum, Getty, Granger Collection, Harley-Davidson, iStock Photo, Jeff Schweitzer, Library of Congress, Mile High Maps, Mountain High Maps, North Wind Picture Archives, One Mile Up, Peter Arnold, Rich Evenhouse, University of Wisconsin-Stout, and Wisconsin Historical Society.
Statistics: State population statistics taken from 2008 U.S. Census Bureau estimates. City and town population statistics taken from July 1, 2007, U.S. Census Bureau estimates. Land and water area statistics taken from 2000 Census, U.S. Census Bureau.

Manufactured with paper containing at least 10% post-consumer waste

Library of Congress Cataloging-in-Publication Data

Ollhoff, Jim, 1959-
  Wisconsin / Jim Ollhoff.
     p. cm. -- (The United States)
  Includes index.
  ISBN 978-1-60453-686-7
  1. Wisconsin--Juvenile literature. I. Title.

  F5810.3.O45 2009
  977.5--dc22
                          2008052883

Table of Contents

The Badger State

People have lived in Wisconsin for thousands of years. Many different cultures and groups live in the state.

Wisconsin was home to the Native American tribes of Ojibwa, Menominee, Ho-Chunk, and others. The word "Wisconsin" may come from the Ojibwa language. It may have been their term for the Wisconsin River.

Wisconsin is often called America's Dairyland because it produces so much milk, cheese, and butter.

In the early 1800s, people came to Wisconsin to work in the lead mines. Sometimes they dug homes in the sides of hills. The miners, it was said, lived like badgers. To this day, Wisconsin's nickname is "The Badger State." It reminds people of the importance of mining in the state's early history.

Wisconsin is often called America's Dairyland.

Quick Facts

Name: The name "Wisconsin" possibly comes from an Ojibwa word describing the Wisconsin River.

State Capital: Madison, population 228,775

Date of Statehood: May 29, 1848 (30th state)

Population: 5,627,967 (20th-most populous state)

Area (Total Land and Water): 65,498 square miles (169,639 sq km), 23rd-largest state

Largest City: Milwaukee, population 602,191

Nicknames: The Badger State or America's Dairyland

Motto: Forward

State Bird: Robin

State Flower: Wood Violet

State Rock: Red Granite

State Tree: Sugar Maple

State Song: "On Wisconsin!"

Highest Point: Timm's Hill, 1,951 feet (595 m)

Lowest Point: Lake Michigan, 579 feet (176 m)

Average July Temperature: 71°F (22°C)

Record High Temperature: 114°F (46°C), in Wisconsin Dells on July 13, 1936

Average January Temperature: 17°F (-8°C)

Record Low Temperature: -55°F (-48°C) in Couderay on February 4, 1996

Average Annual Precipitation: 32 inches (81 cm)

Number of U.S. Senators: 2

Number of U.S. Representatives: 8

Timm's Hill

U.S. Postal Service Abbreviation: WI

Geography

More than two million years ago, glaciers crept over the land. Over a period of hundreds of thousands of years, as the glaciers moved forward and retreated, they created the surface of the land we see today. Some glaciers bulldozed huge areas of land, leaving flat plains or softly rolling hills, as in southern Wisconsin. As glaciers retreated, they left clay, sediment, and silt, creating fertile soil for farming. Some melting glaciers created huge lakes such as Lake Michigan and Lake Superior.

Most rock in Wisconsin is sedimentary rock. This is rock that is formed when once-living materials, dirt, and small pieces of other rocks compress together.

LAKE SUPERIOR

MICHIGAN

Lac Vieux
Desert

N

0   100 miles
0   100 km

WISCONSIN

Wisconsin River

Eau Claire

Green Bay

94

39

43

Mississippi River

Lake
Winnebago

Green
Lake

90

MINNESOTA

LAKE MICHIGAN

MICHIGAN

IOWA

Wisconsin River

Madison

94

Milwaukee

90

Kenosha

ILLINOIS

Wisconsin's total land and water area is 65,498 square miles (169,639 sq km). It is the 23rd-largest state. The state capital is Madison.

In the north part of Wisconsin, igneous rock is very common. Igneous rock is formed by the cooling of molten magma, often blown out of the earth by volcanoes.

Above the Wisconsin rock is a thick layer of fertile soil, deposited by melting glacial runoff. Almost half of Wisconsin, specifically the northern half, is covered by forest. Large areas of northern Wisconsin are designated as national forests. In the southern part of the state, Wisconsin has rich farmland.

Chequamegon National Forest in northern Wisconsin covers 858,400 acres (347,382 ha). It is larger than the state of Rhode Island.

Wisconsin has more than 15,000 lakes. The largest inland lake is Lake Winnebago, covering 215 square miles (557 sq km). The deepest natural inland lake is Green Lake, at 237 feet (72 m) deep. The longest river is the Wisconsin River. It begins its journey from a lake called Lac Vieux Desert on the northeast corner of Wisconsin, bordering Michigan. The river snakes a path through Wisconsin that is more than 430 miles (692 km) long, emptying into the Mississippi River on the southwest corner of the state.

An overlook shows where the Wisconsin and Mississippi Rivers meet.

Climate and Weather

Being a northern state, Wisconsin has long, cold winters. The temperature in January averages about 12 degrees Fahrenheit (-11°C) in the north side

A Wisconsin road after a heavy snowstorm.

of the state, to about 22 degrees Fahrenheit (-6°C) in the south side of the state. Winter snowfall averages more than 100 inches (254 cm) in the far north, and about 30 inches (76 cm) in the south. The coldest temperature ever recorded was in Couderay in 1996, at -55 degrees Fahrenheit (-48°C).

Wisconsin's summers are warm. Temperatures in July average about 69 degrees Fahrenheit (21°C) in the northern part of the state. July temperatures on the south side average about 73 degrees (23°C). The hottest temperature ever recorded was 114 degrees Fahrenheit (46°C), in Wisconsin Dells in 1936. The north side of the state averages about 30 summer thunderstorms per year. The southern part of the state gets about 40 thunderstorms per year.

A Wisconsin thunderstorm.

Spring is a beautiful season when plants bloom. In the autumn, leaves change to a stunning range of colors.

Annual rainfall is about 32 inches (81 cm), falling mostly between May and October.

Plants and Animals

Canada geese
are plentiful in Wisconsin.

At one time, before the Europeans came, forests covered 85 percent of the state. In the 1700s and 1800s, Wisconsin had an abundance of caribou, moose, bison, wolves, cougars, elk, and deer. Early explorers reported that birds were so thick that they "blocked the sun from the sky."

In the 1830s, Europeans began to flood the state. The human population changed Wisconsin. As towns were built, people began hunting, farming, and cutting down trees. Many animals lost their homes. Some animals, such as the caribou and moose, were soon gone from the state.

After much of Wisconsin's forests were cut down in the 1800s, trees were replanted in the 1900s, bringing back much of the forestland.

Lumber mills were big business in Wisconsin in the early years. Lumberjacks cut down many of the state's trees. Since then, the forests have made a comeback. Today, about 46 percent of the state is forest, mostly in the north. The forests are filled with pine, ash, birch, oak, and maple trees.

Wisconsin still has a rich diversity of animals. Black bears, coyotes, porcupines, beavers, otters, and eagles find their homes in the thick forests of the north. Deer, rabbits, skunks, woodchucks, squirrels, and chipmunks can be found all over the state. By 1960, wolves were gone from the state. But legislators passed laws to protect them. Today, wolves have made a comeback in the very northern part of Wisconsin.

In the rivers and lakes, fish are found in abundance. Common types of fish include sunfish, trout, bass, walleye, and northern pike.

White-Tailed Deer

Black Bear

Porcupine

Rabbit

History

People have lived in the Wisconsin area since about 10,000 BC. When the Europeans arrived, the state was populated by many Native American tribes.

With a gun in each hand, French explorer Jean Nicolet landed on the Wisconsin shore in 1634.

Wisconsin had the Ojibwa (Chippewa), Sauk, Menominee, Ho-Chunk (the French called them Winnebago), and others.

The first European to see Wisconsin may have been the French explorer Étienne Brulé, who explored Lake Superior as early as 1622. The person who usually gets credit as being the first European on Wisconsin soil was explorer Jean Nicolet. He came ashore at Green Bay in 1634.

In the 1600s and 1700s, traders and trappers continued to come and go out of present-day Wisconsin. The French claimed control of the area during those early years. In 1763, the French gave control to the British. The British gave control to the United States in 1783. However, the Menominee, Sauk, Fox, Ho-Chunk, and Chippewa nations wanted control of the land too, since they had been living there for hundreds of years.

Trappers watching for otter in Wisconsin.

Black Hawk led the Sauk and Fox Indian tribes as they fought for their land against the United States Army. The Native Americans lost their battle in 1832 during what became known as the Black Hawk War.

After years of fighting, several tribes lost the battle over their lands in 1832. That year, the U.S. Army killed many Native Americans in the Black Hawk War. Also, smallpox, a disease brought in by settlers, killed thousands of Native Americans. In many tribes, half of the people died from smallpox. In Wisconsin, a lot of Native Americans gave up. Most were forced to move away.

This opened the door for settlers. The population skyrocketed. In 1820, the number of white settlers was 651. In 1850, the number of white settlers was more than 300,000.

Many immigrants rushed to work in the lead mines in the southwest corner of the state. It was sometimes called the "lead rush." In the 1830s and 1840s, Wisconsin produced half of the lead used in the United States.

The Martin Mine in Benton, Wisconsin, in 1915.

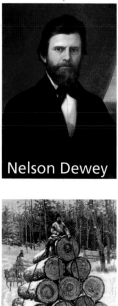

Nelson Dewey

In 1836, Congress created Wisconsin Territory. On May 29, 1848, Congress declared Wisconsin a state. It was the 30th state in the Union. Businessman and lawyer Nelson Dewey was the first governor of the state.

Lumbering became important in the 1870s. Much of the northern forests had been clear-cut by the commercial lumbering companies. Mining for iron began in the 1880s. Millions of tons of iron ore were shipped in the years to come.

The 1920s were good times for the United States. People were shocked when the stock market crashed in 1929. This created the Great Depression. Many people were out of work and out of money.

Milwaukee was hit very hard. Nearly 75 percent of the city's population lost their jobs. A severe drought hit the Midwest in the 1930s, making it even harder for farmers to earn a living.

Toward the end of the 1930s, Wisconsin's economy began to improve. World War II also helped the economy. Wisconsin's farms produced needed dairy products for the country. When World War II ended in 1945, Wisconsin continued to lead the nation in dairy product production for 50 years.

Hundreds of cans of milk are unloaded at the Pet Milk Company in 1945.

Did You Know?

Disease-Free Air!

When Wisconsin was declared a territory in 1836, the new Wisconsin government wanted to attract settlers. They started to distribute brochures and place advertisements in newspapers. Wisconsin Territory even opened an office in New York City to get people to move to the state.

The brochures and advertisements promised cheap land and a new start on the frontier. The brochures also promised "disease-free air." In those days, they believed that diseases were caused by bad air from living in the city. For areas that were overpopulated, like New York City or parts of Europe, the promise of "disease-free air" was a powerful reason to move to Wisconsin.

Settlers streamed in by the thousands, mostly from New York. Immigrants flooded the state, too, mostly from Germany.

In the late 1830s, thousands of people moved to Wisconsin Territory, attracted by ads that offered cheap land and "disease-free air."

People

Gene Wilder (1933–) is an Emmy Award-winning actor who was born in Milwaukee, Wisconsin. He studied acting at the University of Iowa. He went on to star in very popular movies, including *Willy Wonka and the Chocolate Factory* (1972), *Young Frankenstein* (1974), and *Blazing Saddles* (1974). He continues to be active as a producer and writer, as well as an actor.

Speed skater **Eric Heiden** (1958–) was born in Madison, Wisconsin. In the 1980 Winter Olympics, he won five gold medals in speed skating. He set four Olympic records and one world record. He is often considered to be the best speed skater in history. He started college at the University of Wisconsin in Madison. He eventually moved to California to become a medical doctor. He continues to work as a doctor with the United States speed skating teams.

Magician and escape artist **Harry Houdini** (1874–1926) was born in Hungary, but moved to Appleton, Wisconsin, when he was young. He always told people that Appleton was his hometown. Houdini started as a magician, but became famous as a person who could escape handcuffs and straitjackets. He thrilled audiences by being shackled with chains, placed in a locked crate, dropped into water, and then quickly escaping. A popular showman, he died on October 31, 1926, probably from an infected appendix.

Author **Laura Ingalls Wilder** (1867–1957) was born near the village of Pepin, Wisconsin, on February 7, 1867. She moved frequently. When Laura was 15, she became a schoolteacher. At age 18, she married Almanzo Wilder. Many years later, Laura wrote down her childhood stories. Her books, such as *Little House on the Prairie,* became instant classics.

John Muir (1838–1914) came to America  from Scotland in 1849. His family lived on a farm near Portage, Wisconsin. Muir attended the University of Wisconsin. He loved land and nature. Muir urged the U.S. government to create protected areas and a careful forest policy. In the late 1880s, Congress created national parks and national forests. Muir founded the Sierra Club. In 1908, President Theodore Roosevelt set aside land in California and named it Muir Woods National Monument.

Cities

Milwaukee is in southeast Wisconsin, along the shores of Lake Michigan. It is the state's largest city, with 602,191 people. In the late 1700s, the area became a fur trading center. In the early 1800s, three settlers bought large amounts of land there, and began to build a city. Milwaukee's importance grew as a shipping center, and then a national railroad hub. Breweries and manufacturing plants created many jobs. Today, Milwaukee has a varied economy. The city is home to many cultural festivals and museums.

Madison is the capital of Wisconsin, and the state's second-largest city, with a population of 228,775. It lies in the south central part of the state. The Native American tribes of Sauk, Fox, and Ho-Chunk were early inhabitants of the area. Judge James Doty founded the city in 1836. He named the city after President James Madison, who died in the summer of 1836. Today, Madison is an agricultural center for many of Wisconsin's products. Dairy products, cash crops, and livestock are sold here. It is the home to many manufacturing factories. The University of Wisconsin is also one of the city's main employers. Madison is full of bike paths, parks, lakes, and museums.

Green Bay is in the eastern part of the state on the shores of Lake Michigan. Its population is 100,781. The first European to explore the region was probably Jean Nicolet. In 1634, he named the area La Baie Verta, which is French for "The Green Bay." The area's water had a green tint. A fur trading post was soon established. In 1754, Green Bay was incorporated as a town. Today, one of the city's primary industries is papermaking. Food processing, health care, tourism, and agriculture are also important to the economy. The city is famous as the home of the Green Bay Packers football team, which was founded in 1919.

The Green Bay Packers play their home games at Lambeau Field in Green Bay.

Kenosha Public Museum

Kenosha is located in the very southeast corner of the state. It might be called a southern suburb of Milwaukee, or a northern suburb of Chicago, Illinois. It is the fourth-largest city in the state, with a population of 96,265. Archeologists found very old settlements in the area. The Kenosha Public Museum has woolly mammoth bones that are about 12,500 years old. The bones show marks that may have been made by ancient human hunters using stone tools.

Transportation

In the 1600s, the first European explorers and trappers canoed the Great Lakes. As fur trading increased, the traders began using the area's rivers.

Railroads were the next mode of transportation. In 1857, the first train traveled from Lake Michigan to the Mississippi River, all the way across Wisconsin. These railroads gave farmers additional places to sell their products. It also gave immigrants an easier way to come to the state. Today, there are more than 3,400 miles (5,472 km) of railroad tracks in Wisconsin.

When automobiles became popular, the state's roads were paved. Often, roads were created right over the horse trails. Today, there are about 12,000 miles (19,312 km)

US Highway 42 in Door County.

of state and interstate highways, and more than 100,000 miles (160,934 km) of local roads and streets.

There are many highways throughout Wisconsin. Interstate I-90 connects Madison with the Minnesota cities of Minneapolis and St. Paul. Interstates I-43 and I-94 connect Chicago, Illinois, to Green Bay, by way of Milwaukee. Interstate I-39 runs north and south.

There are more than 130 public airports in Wisconsin. The state's largest is General Mitchell International Airport in Milwaukee.

Natural Resources

The people of Wisconsin work to protect and enjoy the beauty of their state. Wisconsin has about 100 state parks, wildlife areas, state forests, and state recreation areas. There are also hundreds of miles of bike trails, and more than 2,730 miles (4,394 km) of hiking trails.

Black River Delta near La Crosse, Wisconsin.

Wisconsin has more than 15,000 lakes. There are also about 84,000 miles (135,185 km) of rivers and streams. That's enough miles to circle the planet three times.

A fisherman lays on the ice next to his catch, a 72-inch (183 cm), 102-pound (46-k) sturgeon he caught on Lake Winnebago.

Wisconsin's many lakes and forests create a home for plenty of wildlife. This makes hunting and fishing popular pastimes.

Commercial fishing is important for the state. Fish farmers raise trout, walleye, muskies, northern pike, bass, and bluegills for restaurants. There are more than 350 fish farms in the state.

Wisconsin's climate, rich soil, and flat ground make it a good place for farming. The state is always among the top producers in the nation of milk, cheese, and butter.

Industry

Agriculture is a big industry in Wisconsin. There are 78,463 farms in the state. More than 99 percent of these are

A cranberry farm.

family-owned farms. Wisconsin agriculture is mostly dairy farming. Dairy products, including milk, butter, and cheese, bring in more than $4.5 billion per year. About 55 percent of all farm products are dairy related.

Wisconsin farmers also raise cattle, hogs, and poultry. Wisconsin leads the nation in the production of ginseng and cranberries. Corn and snap beans are also important.

Manufacturing provides many jobs in Wisconsin. Milwaukee is a major center for machinery production.

Wisconsin firms lead the nation in the production of small engines for industrial equipment. Wisconsin is one of the chief producers of paper and paper products in the United States.

Harley-Davidson's headquarters is in Milwaukee, Wisconsin.

Many well-known firms are based in Wisconsin. The Harley-Davidson Motor Company has headquarters in Milwaukee. Johnsonville Sausage, S.C. Johnson & Son, GE Healthcare Clinical Systems, and Trek Bicycle Corporation are all companies in Wisconsin.

Tourism is also a major industry in Wisconsin. The state's many parks and forests get about 14 million visitors each year. Skiers and snowmobilers flock to the state in the winter, bringing millions of dollars in tourism.

Sports

It is hard to get very far in Wisconsin without hearing about the Green Bay Packers. They are a professional football team based in the city of Green Bay. They are the last of the small town teams, which were common

Packers fans are fondly known as "Cheeseheads."

in the 1920s. Curly Lambeau (1898-1965) helped form the team in 1919, and became the Packers' first coach. The team currently plays at Green Bay's Lambeau Field, named after the founder. The Packers have won more championships than any other team.

Besides football, Wisconsin has other professional sports teams as well. The Milwaukee Brewers play baseball, and the Milwaukee Bucks play basketball.

The Wisconsin Badgers, of the University of Wisconsin-Madison, includes men's and women's championship teams in hockey, football, and basketball, plus many other sports.

A scuba-diver explores the wreck of the *Wisconsin*. The steamer sank off Kenosha in 1929.

Besides watching sports, there is plenty to do in Wisconsin. Thousands of miles of hiking and biking paths crisscross the state. Divers swim in the Great Lakes, exploring shipwrecks from as far back as the 1800s.

Hunting is a big pastime in Wisconsin. The state's lakes provide opportunity for sailing and waterskiing. Winter sports include cross-country skiing, snowshoeing, snowmobiling, and even dogsledding.

Entertainment

Wisconsin has many festivals. Oktoberfest celebrates the German traditions. Milwaukee's Festa Italiana celebrates those of Italian heritage, with music, food, and other activities. Finding Kunu is a Ho-Chunk Native American celebration. The Swiss offer the William Tell Festival in New Glarus. Norwegians hold the Syttende Mai festival in Stoughton.

A dancer at Milwaukee's Indian Summer Festival.

A cheese carver at the Great Wisconsin Cheese Festival.

There are museums of every type in Wisconsin, from small county museums to nationally known galleries of art and history. There is even the Mustard Museum in Mount Horeb, west of Madison.

Milwaukee's Summerfest is one of the nation's largest music festivals, with hundreds of performers. Wisconsin Dells is one of the most popular tourist sites in the state. It is known for its water parks, rides, and family fun.

A man cools off on a water park ride.

Wisconsin has just about every kind of attraction imaginable. It's possible to hear German polka bands in the morning, and Native American drums in the afternoon. With museums, events, zoos, and other attractions, Wisconsin has something for everyone.

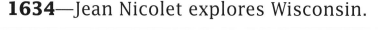

Timeline

1634—Jean Nicolet explores Wisconsin.

1673—French explorers Marquette and
Joliet try to find a water route from
Lake Michigan to the Mississippi River.

1764—Charles Langlade moves to Green
Bay. He founds the first permanent
settlement in Wisconsin.

1832—Black Hawk War. Many Native
Americans are killed or forced to leave
their land.

1848—Wisconsin becomes the 30th state
in the Union.

1857—Railroad completed from Milwaukee to Prairie du Chien.

1861-1865—96,000 Wisconsin soldiers serve in Civil War. 12,216 die in conflict.

1941-1945—320,000 Wisconsin residents serve in the U.S. military in World War II.

1958—University of Wisconsin scientist Joshua Lederberg is awarded the Nobel Prize for medicine.

1980—Eric Heiden of Madison wins five gold medals in speedskating at the Winter Olympics.

1997—The Green Bay Packers win Super Bowl XXXI.

Glossary

Black Hawk War—A series of battles in 1832 between white settlers and Sauk and Fox Native Americans, under the leadership of Black Hawk.

Glacier—A massive, slow moving river of ice typically formed from compacted layers of snow. During the ice age, glaciers covered much of present-day Wisconsin.

Great Depression—A time in American history beginning in 1929 and lasting for several years when many businesses failed across the country and millions of people lost their jobs.

Green Bay Packers—The professional football team, originating in the city of Green Bay. They were established in 1919.

Igneous Rock—Rock formed by the cooling of molten magma.

Immigrant—A person settling in a new country, after leaving their former homeland.

Lake Michigan—One of the Great Lakes, with Michigan on its eastern shore, and Wisconsin on its western shore.

Lake Superior—The largest of the Great Lakes, bordering Michigan, Wisconsin, Minnesota, and Canada.

Sedimentary Rock—Rock that is formed by a slow process of pressing together small particles such as sand and silt.

University of Wisconsin—A statewide system of universities. It was created by the legislature in 1848, and began the first class with 17 students in 1849. Today it has 13 campuses.

World War II—A conflict across the world, lasting from 1939-1945. The United States entered the war in December 1941.

Index

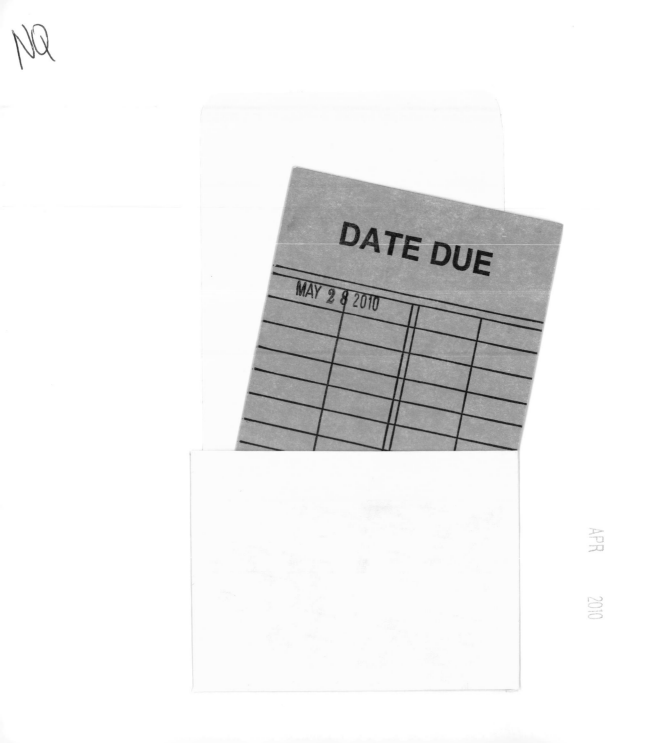